Table of Contents

Anger is a normal human emotion. It is neither good nor bad.

How people manage their anger can make the emotion either useful or harmful.

Feeling angry involves both the body and the mind. Physical changes prepare the body to act. The mind decides how the person will respond.

Factors that influence how much anger affects a person include sex, race, cultural background, family background, self-esteem, and age.

Chapter 1

What Is Anger?

ALANA, AGE 17

Alana parks in front of Rosie's home and honks. No Rosie. Alana honks harder. Still no Rosie. "Come on, girl," Alana mutters. "We're going to be late for school."

Rosie is Alana's best friend, but she can be annoying. "She's never on time," Alana thinks. "If she doesn't come out in the next 30 seconds, I'm leaving." Alana drums her fingers on the steering wheel. She can feel herself getting tense. Her cheeks feel hot.

Just then, Rosie runs out and hops in the car. "Let's go," she says, as if nothing is wrong. Alana cannot believe her!

Alana is angry. Anger is a normal human emotion, or feeling. Everyone experiences anger, although not always in the same way. Anger can range from annoyance to full-blown rage.

People can choose how to manage their anger. For example, Alana might do several things. She could lash out at Rosie. This approach risks damage to their friendship. Another choice is that Alana could pretend she is not bothered and say nothing. Most likely, this will make Alana feel resentful. Alana also could wait until she is calmer. Then she could tell Rosie how she feels and ask her to be on time. The last approach has the best chance of solving Alana's problem.

Anger: A Two-Sided Emotion

You may think anger is bad or dangerous. Many people do. However, anger is neither good nor bad. What counts is how people manage their anger. The feeling of anger and a person's response to it are separate things.

Constructive Anger

Anger can be constructive. Anger can warn you of problems so you can take action. It can protect you from danger and abuse. For example, if someone breaks into your locker and steals your CD player, you will probably feel angry. In fact, if you don't get mad, your friends might wonder why.

Instead of raging, however, you can let your anger spur you to find a solution to your problem. You might vow to change your locker combination. You might ask a teacher to help you track down the thief. Anger is powerful. It can give you the energy to accomplish your goals.

A lot of good things have happened because people used their anger constructively. Here are a few:

Civil Rights Movement

Americans With Disabilities Act

Mothers Against Drunk Driving

Anger also is useful in changing situations that are unjust or wrong. Angry people can band together to right the wrong. That is what happened when two high school seniors died in a car accident caused by a drunk driver. The classmates of the students who died were angry about the senseless deaths. They started a chapter of SADD at their school.

The initials SADD can stand for Students Against Destructive Decisions or Students Against Drinking and Driving. The SADD members tried to persuade politicians to pass tougher penalties for drunk drivers. They e-mailed their state government officials and wrote letters to the local newspaper. The students also held a service to remind themselves and others of their friends. The service drew more public attention to the problem of drunk driving.

Destructive Anger

Anger also can be destructive. Uncontrolled anger can lead to broken relationships and lost opportunities and respect. It also can result in low self-esteem and health problems. Extreme anger can lead a person to violence, criminal behavior, and even to suicide, or taking one's own life.

Uncontrolled anger can cause problems in the workplace. An inability to manage their anger is the number one reason qualified people get bypassed for promotions.

What Happens When You're Angry?

Anger begins with a threat to your sense of well-being. People or situations outside of you present external threats. Your own thoughts or memories also can trigger anger. Internal threats like worrying about personal problems or recalling a past experience can make you angry.

Your Body's Response

Your nervous system recognizes the threat and automatically springs into action. It prepares your body to defend itself against the threat. Your defense starts in your adrenal glands. These glands are located at the top of each kidney. They release adrenaline and other hormones, the chemicals that control body functions.

Adrenaline causes your heart to beat faster. It makes your blood pressure rise and quickens your breathing. It dilates, or expands, your pupils. Your liver sends extra sugar into your bloodstream. The sugar is used for energy. Blood flows away from your internal organs and into your muscles. You are now supercharged and ready to respond.

Your Mind's Response

Both people and animals have defense systems built into their body. However, in humans anger arouses the mind as well as the body. To experience anger, your mind must recognize that you are being threatened. Your mind also must be able to blame someone or something.

In other words, anger is all in how a person interprets an event or situation. Something that causes anger in one person may not affect another person. It is important to realize that only you can control your anger. Controlling your anger means that anger cannot control you.

Somebody bumped Andy from behind while he stood in the cafeteria line. Andy felt himself tense up. He whirled to see who had knocked into him. It was a kid he had never seen before. Andy decided the bump was an accident. He turned back to his friends.

ANDY, AGE 15

A few minutes later, it happened again. This time a kid Andy knew and did not like bumped him. Andy decided the kid had bumped him on purpose. Angry, Andy put his fist in the kid's face. The two had to be pulled apart to stop the fight.

Hot as a Chili Pepper, Cool as a Cucumber

Ray gets mad at the drop of a hat, but nothing seems to bother Joel. Why do people show anger so differently? Some possible reasons are sex, race, and cultural background. Other reasons may be family background, self-esteem, and age.

Sex, Race, and Cultural Background

A person's sex, race, and cultural background all contribute to his or her emotional makeup. People's differences make them each unique members of the human race. Sometimes, however, people are treated unfairly because of their sex, race, or cultural differences. Such negative experiences can produce anger. How people express their anger can differ depending on their emotional makeup and experiences.

Family Background

Children learn from the example their parents set. Some parents yell, swear, and slam doors when they are angry. Their children may be likely to act the same way. At the other extreme, some parents find it hard to show their feelings. Their children may learn to hide anger.

Self-Esteem

High self-esteem and feeling good about oneself usually go hand in hand. People with high self-esteem who feel good about themselves can manage anger constructively. They generally take criticism and frustration in stride.

Controlling anger can be a challenge for teens because:

The same hormones that cause a teen's body to grow and change also affect his or her moods. This can make it more difficult for teens to remain calm.

Most teens strive to become independent. This can lead to conflict with parents and other adults.

Today's teens live in an increasingly angry society.

Age

A person's age may influence how he or she expresses anger. Young people are still learning to manage anger and may have more angry outbursts than adults.

Points to Consider

What do you think of when you hear the word *anger*?

Think of a time when you used your anger in an unhealthy way. Then think of a time when you used anger in a healthy way. Do you feel the same way when you think of these times? Why or why not?

Is destructive anger a problem in your school? Explain.

How have you or people you know used anger to help others?

People manage anger using one of three main styles. Some people use a combination of styles.

People with passive anger hold anger in. This can lead to loss of self-esteem, poor relationships, and long-term health problems.

People with aggressive anger overreact to anger. This can lead to loss of respect from others, broken relationships, and long-term health problems.

People with assertive anger express anger without hurting themselves or others. They attempt to use anger to solve problems.

Chapter 2

Anger Styles

People handle their anger in different ways. Three main anger styles are passive, aggressive, and assertive. You may use one of these styles by itself or in combination with another style. See if you recognize yourself and people you know in the following descriptions.

The Avoiders—Passive Anger

Cole's girlfriend, Lisa, broke up with him. Cole felt hurt and

COLE, AGE 17

angry, but he told everyone that he didn't care. Shortly after the breakup, Cole's friend Miles began dating Lisa. Cole's blood boiled whenever he saw Miles and Lisa together. However, Cole never let on that he was jealous.

Cole's anger style is passive. People with this style stuff their feelings inside. They try to avoid their anger, and they never let others see it. They do not act outwardly on their anger. They may blame themselves for something that wasn't their fault. People with passive anger may be unaware of just how angry they are.

Why People Use Passive Anger

People who use a passive style may believe that anger is a sign of weakness. They may think that polite, sensible people do not get angry. They may fear that showing anger will cause others to reject them. Often, people with passive anger want to avoid conflict. They think that never showing anger is a way to maintain peaceful relations with others.

Dangers of Passive Anger

A passive anger style keeps the peace, but at great personal cost. The needs of passively angry people are unmet when they constantly give in to others. This can lead to feelings of resentment and a loss of self-esteem.

Healthy relationships depend on honest sharing of feelings. Passively angry people find it hard to share feelings. People who bottle up anger too long can explode into violence. Also, over time, passive anger can result in depression, stomach problems, chronic or long-lasting pain, and other problems.

Anger Management

"Last week I was out with my friends. I blew up when one of the guys laughed at my shirt. Afterward I felt really stupid. It wasn't that big a deal. I wonder what they think of me now."
—Brandon, age 17

Passive-Aggressive Anger

People with passive anger may find sneaky ways to attack others. They may scowl, criticize, or make sarcastic comments. They may show up too late to get to a concert or other planned activity. If they are angry at a parent, they may "lose" telephone or e-mail messages for that parent. These indirect attacks are part of a passive-aggressive anger style.

The Exploders—Aggressive Anger

Alexi had a part in the school play. One day at rehearsal the drama teacher criticized Alexi's performance. Alexi got mad. She yelled at the teacher, threw down her script, and stalked off stage. The rest of the cast rolled their eyes and shook their heads.

ALEXI, AGE 16

Alexi's anger style is aggressive. People with this style explode in anger. They may yell, slam doors, break objects, and name-call. They may even shove, pinch, bite, and hit. People with aggressive anger often want revenge. They want to get back at the person they believe wronged them.

People with aggressive anger may become enraged easily. They may be overly sensitive to criticism. They may be impatient. They may have difficulty handling everyday inconveniences like traffic jams. They might blow up when something prevents them from doing what they want to do.

Aggressive anger usually comes and goes quickly. People with aggressive anger usually feel relief after exploding.

Dangers of Aggressive Anger

Aggressive anger does not solve problems. It can damage personal relationships. Someone with aggressive anger may feel better after exploding, but the people around the person may feel hurt. They even may be afraid of the person who explodes. Growing evidence shows that uncontrolled anger is a risk factor for heart disease and stroke.

Deliberate and Addictive Anger

Aggressive anger may take different forms. One form is deliberate anger. This is when people act angry to get something they want. For example, gang members use anger to intimidate, or scare, other people. They hope to gain and keep control. Children and teens may have outbursts of anger, or temper tantrums. They hope to force their parents to give in to their demands.

Myth: It is healthy to let off steam by screaming and punching things when you are angry.

Fact: In the past, mental health counselors recommended that people vent their anger. However, now most experts on anger say that "letting it rip" does not get rid of anger. Instead, venting anger trains people to be angrier. Angry outbursts become a habit.

Another form of aggressive anger is addictive anger. Some people actually enjoy being angry. They like the feeling they get from their anger.

The Thinkers—Assertive Anger

PAULETTE, AGE 15

Paulette discovered that her little brother had been messing with her stuff again. She was furious. Her first impulse was to go to his room and throw his baseball card collection on the floor. Then she thought again. She wondered why he kept bothering her things.

Paulette sat her brother down for a chat. She told him how she felt about having her personal space invaded. Her brother seemed to understand. Paulette thought her brother might be looking for attention. She decided to spend more time with him. After their conversation, Paulette's brother stopped going into her room.

Paulette's anger style is assertive. People with this style try to keep their anger from reaching an explosive level. They assert, or stick up for, themselves without putting the other person on the defensive. They explain why they are angry, and they try to understand the other person's point of view. People with assertive anger think about the best way to manage their feelings.

Advantages of Assertive Anger

Assertive anger has several advantages over passive-aggressive anger. People who use anger assertively seek to solve problems. As a result, they are more likely to get what they need. Also, their personal relationships have a better chance of surviving. They release their anger without hurting themselves or others.

You may have heard of Type A and Type B personalities. Type A people are always on the move. Type B people are more relaxed. Some researchers now have identified a Type H personality. Type H people are chronically hostile. Hostile means angry, distrustful, and critical. Researchers say more study is needed on this personality type.

Points to Consider

Which anger style fits you most of the time? Give an example of when you handled your anger in this way. What was the outcome?

How do you feel when you are with someone who is using passive anger? aggressive anger? assertive anger?

Which anger style fits your family? Why do you think it fits your family?

Think of a situation that might cause you to become angry. For example, you have just had a haircut. You asked for a trim. The stylist gave you a buzz cut. How would you handle your anger in a passive style? an aggressive style? an assertive style?

Chapter Overview

Anger triggers are events or situations that set off anger. Anger triggers vary from person to person.

Types of anger triggers include physical or emotional hurts, frustrations, injustices, and annoyances.

Anger triggers provoke uncomfortable feelings such as powerlessness and fear.

One of the best ways to control anger is to change negative and irrational, or unreasonable, thinking. Others are avoiding the trigger, planning ahead, finding alternative solutions, changing the timing, and learning to ignore the trigger.

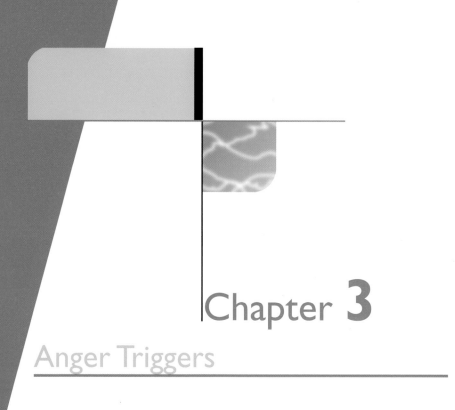

Chapter **3**

Anger Triggers

Not everyone gets upset about the same things. Something that makes you mad may not bother your friend. What upsets your friend may make no difference to you. Knowing what triggers your anger and why it does so can help you manage your feelings.

Types of Anger Triggers
Four types of anger triggers are physical or emotional hurts, frustrations, injustices, and annoyances.

Anger triggers can vary from culture to culture. For example, in some cultures a teacher might be annoyed if you did not maintain eye contact. In other cultures, a teacher might be angered if you did.

Physical or Emotional Hurts

Examples of physical hurts include getting hit, slapped, poked, grabbed, shoved, or kicked. Examples of emotional hurts include insults, name-calling, teasing, put-downs, and rejection. Inappropriate sexual touching can be both a physical and an emotional hurt.

Frustrations

Frustrations occur when you can't reach a goal or do something the way you want. Other people may oppose your efforts. Often, however, your own inability to do something leads to frustration. Then frustration can turn to self-anger. Constant self-anger can lead to serious consequences such as low self-esteem or depression.

RENA, AGE 13

Rena wanted to in-line skate like the guys on her block. They could glide, turn, and do fancy jumps. Rena kept falling when she tried a stunt. After falling many times, Rena gave up. She pulled off her skates and threw them as far as she could. "I can't do anything," she thought.

Injustices

An injustice is an act or situation that is unfair or that threatens someone's rights. You can get angry about injustices directed at you or at someone else. Here are a few examples:

You get blamed for something you did not do.

You have to do more chores around the house than your brother or sister.

You told a friend a personal secret. Your friend told your secret to everyone else.

You see your classmates tease a student with a disability.

Annoyances

Annoyances are the everyday things that can upset you. Here are a few examples:

You're in a hurry, and you break a shoelace.

The person in the line behind you continuously snaps gum.

Your friend keeps interrupting you when you're talking.

To help you discover your anger triggers, complete this sentence seven times with seven different triggers:

I get angry when _____.

Finding the Reason

Thinking about why something triggers your anger is helpful. Maybe the trigger makes you feel powerless or afraid. Jana gets mad when her friends do something without her. She thinks they no longer want to be her friend. Paul gets mad when his friend brags about getting good grades. It makes him feel stupid.

Keeping the Gun From Going Off

You can take steps to stop your anger triggers from working. The following are some methods you can use.

Avoid the Trigger

The most obvious way to control anger is to avoid the trigger. This applies especially to frustrating situations. Decide how important the goal is to you. If it's not that important, find something else to do. If the goal is important, keep trying but avoid criticizing yourself. Take breaks or ask someone to help you.

Change Your Thinking

One of the best ways to manage anger is to change your thinking. Research shows that changing the way you think also changes the way you feel.

Listen to your thoughts. Do you hear yourself saying negative or irrational things about other people or situations? Stop and replace these thoughts with positive ones as in the following example.

Three types of irrational thinking are:

Overgeneralization—making things bigger than they are: "You're always late" or "This machine never works."

Mind reading—assuming you know what another person is thinking: "I know my teacher does not like me."

Labeling—thinking of people in terms of labels and not as human beings: "That moron" or "You jerk."

Replace This Negative:	With This Positive:
"This is the worst thing that's ever happened to me."	"This is a bad situation, but I can get through it. Getting angry won't help things."

You also can apply this thinking technique to your thoughts about yourself. Does your inner voice criticize you or put you down? Such negative thoughts feed self-anger and can be very destructive. Instead, use positive self-talk. Give yourself affirmations, or positive statements about yourself.

Replace This Negative:	With This Positive:
"I can't do anything."	"I may not be the best at basketball, but I am a good softball player."

Plan Ahead

If you know when you are likely to encounter a trigger, plan a way to deal with it. For example, you may want to have a party at your apartment. However, your father sometimes embarrasses you in front of your friends. You might ask your father nicely if he would stay in the background during the party.

Find Alternate Solutions

Another method for dealing with anger triggers is to find alternate solutions. For example, your friend is constantly late when you plan to meet. Try setting the meeting time for earlier than you intend to get there. When your friend arrives, he or she will show up at the time you planned to meet.

Change the Timing

Sometimes changing the timing of an activity such as a family discussion can keep tempers from flaring.

> The minute Khai gets home from school his mother asks
>
> **KHAI, AGE 16**
>
> questions. How was his day? Did he pass his history test? Does he have a lot of homework? This makes Khai mad. He gives short answers and drops in front of the TV.
>
> Khai finally told his mother he needs time to himself when he gets home. After unwinding awhile, Khai is ready to talk.

Learn to Ignore the Trigger

You might simply learn to ignore the trigger. For example, if someone teases you about something, ignore the person. Often the person will stop teasing if you do not respond.

Points to Consider

What are your anger triggers? How could you keep each one from being destructive?

Something about another person might trigger your anger. For example, the person constantly tells you that you are wrong when you know you are not. How could you handle this situation in a healthy way?

Should you reveal your anger triggers to other people? Why or why not?

What affirmations could you give yourself today?

Chapter Overview

Several methods can be used to keep feelings under control.

One important method is to admit your anger. Both the body and mind send signals warning of anger.

It also is important to calm down before saying or doing anything. Acting in the heat of anger can lead you to hurt or embarrass yourself or others. Techniques to relax and activities to make you less tense can reduce anger.

It is easier to deal with a problem when you are calm.

Good communication skills are needed to solve problems.

Chapter **4**

Putting Out the Fire

Managing anger triggers can prevent situations that might lead you to hurt or embarrass yourself or others. Even so, you may find yourself in tense situations from time to time. Then you need additional anger-management methods to help you keep your feelings under control. You can use the following step-by-step emergency plan.

Step 1: Admit You Are Angry

Pay attention to your body. It will warn you when you are getting angry. Some anger signals are:

Pounding heart

Tight muscles

Burning cheeks

Nervous stomach

Loud voice

Pay attention to your mind, too. Negative thoughts such as the following also signal anger:

"What's the matter with that jerk, anyway?"

"Why does everything bad happen to me?"

"I never get to go anywhere."

Get clear on what you're angry about and why. This can guide you as you manage your anger.

Some teens share how they work off anger:

"Write in my journal. I understand what is happening more after I write about it."—Alice, age 15

"Listen to music. To get over being mad I like slow stuff."—Steve, age 16

"Go for a walk. Really far and really fast."—Yolanda, age 15

"Hit my heavy bag a couple of times. Then I laugh." —Sebastian, age 17

Step 2: Calm Down

It's hard to think clearly when you are angry. The first impulse for many angry people is to strike with words or fists. Instead of striking, try to get away from the situation for a while. Then use the following techniques and activities to calm down.

Techniques to Relax

Any one of these simple techniques can help you relax.

Breathe in deeply for four counts, then breathe out for four counts. This helps control your body's response to anger.

Use the old method of counting to 10—or 100, if you need to—before doing or saying anything.

Repeat words or phrases such as "I can handle this," "Don't yell," or "Relax."

Activities to Make You Less Tense

Another way to calm down is to do an activity that will make you less tense. Activities can distract you from thinking about your anger. Exercising, listening to music, or cleaning your room can help you release anger in a physical, nonviolent way. Anger is like fuel. It can give you lots of energy to accomplish something positive.

Step 3: Think About Your Options

You can think about what to do after you are calm. Remember, one option is to do nothing at all. You might base that decision on one of the following reasons:

The event or situation is not serious enough to get worked up over.

Your anger is out of proportion to the event or situation.

You really can't do anything about the situation. Getting angry won't make a worthwhile difference.

Most people receive many invitations to anger. If you accept all the invitations to anger you get, you will battle anger constantly. Remember, walking away from a fight means that you have remained in control. That's something you can be proud of.

Step 4: Solve the Problem

You might decide to change the situation or event that caused your anger. If so, don't wait too long to act. You might lose your urge to do so. Then you might be angry again soon.

Solving the problem often involves talking with another person. That means you will need good communication skills. The next chapter gives you information about those skills.

"Sometimes the littlest thing can tick you off. Like when I was standing in the express lane at the grocery store and the guy ahead of me had a whole cartful of food. I was ready to yell at him. But then I just had to tell myself, 'Hey, this is small stuff. I'm not going to sweat it.'"

—Dori, age 15

DAVID, AGE 14

David was furious. All his friends could stay out late on Friday nights. Why couldn't he? His parents just didn't get it!

David slammed the door as he left the house. He hopped on his bike. During his ride, he decided to talk with his parents again. He would offer to do extra chores if he could stay out later on Friday night. He would promise to let his parents know where he was going.

David felt better when he got back home. He chose a time when he thought his parents were in a good mood. Then he calmly presented his plan. His parents suggested a few things, too. David and his parents worked out a compromise and agreed to try the plan.

Points to Consider

How does your body react when you're angry?

What kinds of things go through your mind when you're angry?

What favorite activities do you use to relax?

Describe a time when you decided not to do anything about a situation that made you angry. Why did you make that decision? What was the outcome?

Chapter Overview

Talking about anger arising from relationships with family members, friends, and classmates can help solve the problem.

Successful communication requires thought and skill. Helpful techniques include *I* statements, active listening, and paying attention to body language.

Mediators can help in some conflicts.

Talking with a trusted adult also can help.

Chapter **5**

Talking It Out

A common source of anger for teens is relationships with family, friends, and classmates. One way to resolve this anger is to talk it out.

Talking out anger has two goals. The first is to solve the problem. The second is to maintain relationships. Try not to focus on who's right or wrong. Instead, try to be assertive and speak up for what you want and need. Instead of focusing on placing blame, work on solutions for the future.

Always show respect for the other person. Try to understand what he or she is thinking and feeling. This is called empathy, or seeing the situation through the other person's eyes. That may help stop anger.

Communicating One-on-One

If possible, talk one-on-one with the other person to prevent further misunderstandings. Communicating when angry requires skill. You can learn this skill with practice. Try to keep the conversation going. That way, you can reach a solution. The following sections suggest some techniques you can use.

Keep Calm

It is important to be calm when talking with the other person. You will be able to think more clearly. You will be less likely to say something hurtful.

Let the other person know in advance that you would like to talk. This will give him or her time to think. Arrange to talk in a safe, quiet place. That will keep the other person from feeling defensive. A defensive person may want to fight back. If your conversation becomes heated, you may need to call a time out.

Spiritual leaders say that forgiveness is a good way to release anger. If someone has hurt you, you might tell him or her that you do not hold a grudge. Apologize if you have said or done something wrong.

Use *I* Statements

Use *I* statements that tell the other person how you feel. An *I* statement does not blame or accuse. Messages that begin with *you,* however, are likely to be blaming. This can make the other person want to fight back. *I* statements encourage conversation. They invite the person to respond with his or her point of view. Here are some ways you can change *you* statements to *I* statements:

You Statements	*I* Statements
"You're always late!"	"I get upset when I have to wait for you."
"You were wrong to tell that story about me."	"I felt embarrassed when you told that story about me."
"You always talk about me behind my back."	"I get mad when people talk about me behind my back."

Practice Active Listening

Use active listening. Show you are listening to what the other person is saying. Nod or say yes from time to time. Do not interrupt. Avoid saying "It can't be that bad" or "I told you so." Comments like these discourage the person from talking.

Paraphrasing is another way to listen actively. Paraphrasing means to restate the other person's views in your own words. For example, you might say, "Do you mean that_____?" or "Are you saying that_____?" If you have not understood, the other person can correct you.

Watch Your Body Language

Your body should convey the same message as your words. Body language means how you hold and move your body. You might say you are willing to talk. However, if you stand with your arms crossed tightly, you may send the opposite message. Your body language should convey respect for the other person. Some examples of body language that show rudeness and hostility are:

Clenched fists

Pointed fingers

Rolling eyes

Scowling

Drumming fingers

Your tone of voice should convey respect as well. A biting, sarcastic tone discourages conversation.

Fifty percent of any message is nonverbal. That means it is without words. Your body language, gestures, facial expression, and tone of voice communicate as much as your words do.

Stick to the Issue

If you are angry because your friend kept you waiting, talk about only that issue. Don't talk about the time your friend borrowed your sweater and did not return it. Bringing up past issues muddies the situation and prevents you from solving the present problem.

Avoid Overgeneralization

Avoid saying things like "You always . . ." or "You never . . . ." These are overgeneralizations. Overgeneralizations communicate that there is no way to solve the problem. That may turn the other person against you.

SONJA, AGE 16, AND MIA, AGE 15

Sonja and Mia are sisters. Their mother is a single parent. She works hard and expects her daughters to do the housework.

Sonja feels she does more than her fair share. She resents that Mia goes off with friends and leaves her with the chores. She kept her feelings to herself until she learned about *I* statements. She decided to try them.

One night as the girls relaxed, Sonja said, "I feel angry when I have to wash clothes and clean the house by myself." Mia's response surprised Sonja. Mia said, "I would do more if you did not act like you wanted to do it all yourself. I feel like you want to be the queen." The sisters started talking. They even decided that it might be fun to do the housework together.

Talking With a Mediator

Sometimes you may not be able to talk one-on-one. Then a mediator may help. A mediator is someone who helps people communicate without favoring one person over the other. Many schools in the United States and Canada train students to be peer mediators. A peer is someone your own age. Peer mediators help classmates resolve conflicts before they get bigger.

ADAM AND CAL, AGE 13

Adam and Cal sat in a conference room at Franklin Middle School. A few minutes later, Clarise joined them. Clarise is a peer mediator. "What's up, guys?" she asked. "Your teacher said you were yelling at each other."

Clarise first heard Adam's side of the story. Next she asked Cal to tell his side. Then she summarized the main points. She asked the guys to think of solutions and choose the one they thought would work the best. After agreeing to a solution, Adam and Cal wrote and signed a contract.

"Man, I'm glad we worked that out," Adam said. Cal nodded.

Talking With a Third Party

One-on-one communication or peer mediation may not be an option. Then a third party may help. A third party is someone who is not involved. A parent, counselor, teacher, spiritual adviser, or other trusted adult can be a third party with good advice.

Some teens talk with a friend when they're angry. This can be helpful or not so helpful. Your friend is likely to take your side. He or she may not offer constructive ways to handle your feelings. You may find yourself getting angry all over again as you tell what happened. If you do talk with a friend, choose someone who can help you solve your problem sensibly.

Points to Consider

Recall a recent situation in which someone made you angry. How might you have handled the situation based on information in this chapter?

Does your school have a peer mediation program? How does it work? If your school does not have a program like this, how could you get one started?

Whom would you ask for help in solving a relationship problem? Why would you choose that person?

Chapter Overview

Good health habits are part of anger management.

Stress and mood-altering substances make people more likely to have angry feelings and thoughts.

Reducing stress helps control anger.

People might use tobacco, alcohol, and other drugs to control or deny their anger. These substances often make angry feelings worse. Alcohol and street drugs also can provoke angry responses.

Chapter **6**

Adding Fuel to the Fire

Health habits play an important role in anger management. People who feel good physically and mentally can handle problems better than people who are tired and stressed. Good health habits include getting enough sleep, eating healthy meals, and exercising. A technique to help you relax, such as meditation, also can help reduce fatigue.

Have you ever blown up at a family member or friend when you were really angry about something that happened at school? Taking your anger out on an innocent bystander is called displacement. Displaced anger hurts feelings all around.

Anger and Stress

Anger and stress go hand in hand. Stress is the feeling people get when they are worried or under pressure. Stress can cause people to become angry.

EVA, AGE 16

Eva lies on her bed and stares at the ceiling. Her mind races with what she has to do. A term paper is due in English. She has a math test on Friday and six chapters to read for history. Then there's soccer practice, her job, and her boyfriend's birthday. Plus, Eva wants to go with friends to a rock concert tonight.

Eva's grandmother comes in and says, "Eva, would you mind taking out the trash?" Eva hits the roof. "I can't do everything!" she shouts. "Take it out yourself!" Later, Eva feels foolish. "Yelling like that was stupid," she thinks. "I really have to get a handle on my temper."

Many anger-management techniques also help you manage stress. Such techniques include identifying and dealing with stress triggers, learning to relax, and staying healthy. Setting priorities and using time wisely also can help keep things from overwhelming you.

Myth: Smoking cigarettes helps people relax.

Fact: Tobacco causes long-term health problems. It does not reduce stress. Instead, it makes bodies work harder and less efficiently.

Anger and Drugs

Some people use tobacco, alcohol, and other drugs to control anger. For example, Kim says that smoking helps her calm down. When she is angry, she walks off, has a cigarette, and then comes back to the situation.

Some people use alcohol and other drugs to numb feelings of anger and pain. Dan's parents fight a lot. Dan says their shouting is not so bad when he is drinking.

Tobacco, alcohol, and other drugs alter a person's mood. They may lift a person's spirits and cause him or her to relax. However, their effect is only temporary. When the good feeling wears off, the problem is still there. In fact, the drugs have the opposite effect after the desired effect is gone. Then a person may feel even more anxiety.

More and more of the drug may be needed to get the same good feeling as before. The person may become addicted. Then he or she has more problems.

Alcohol and street drugs may provoke anger as well as mask it. Alcohol clouds thinking. A person who has been drinking may misinterpret what others say or do. He or she may become furious, even getting into arguments and fights.

JASON, AGE 18

Jason was drinking heavily at a keg party. He thought another guy was looking at his girlfriend, Kris, too much. Enraged, Jason told the guy to stay away from Kris. Then he hit the guy.

Jason could not stop. His friends tried to make him stop and could not. Someone called the police. By the time they arrived, everyone had scattered—except Jason and the battered guy. The police arrested Jason.

Anger Management

"I never knew how angry I was until I got into treatment for alcoholism. My counselor showed me that I drank because I was angry."
—Amanda, age 17

Points to Consider

What causes stress in your life? What could you do to manage stress better?

How would you respond to people who say they smoke to calm their nerves?

What could you do to educate classmates about anger and alcohol?

Chapter
Overview

Chapter
Overview

Some people's anger goes beyond normal. It continues for a long time and is felt deeply. Usually it is destructive.

Causes of excessive, chronic anger include physical and emotional abuse, a traumatic experience, and physical or emotional illness.

Teens with out-of-control anger may withdraw, act out, or seem agitated.

People who can no longer manage their anger need the help of mental health professionals.

Chapter **7**
Bringing in the Bomb Squad

Evan was a reasonably happy teen. He liked school and had a

EVAN, AGE 15

lot of friends. However, during his sophomore year, Evan began acting in angry, violent ways. He argued constantly. He mouthed off to teachers and picked fights.

Evan's parents hoped he would grow out of this behavior. Then one day, Evan's mother found some vicious hate drawings on his desk. Evan admitted he had drawn them. His parents took action. They set up weekly appointments for Evan with a counselor who worked with male teens. Evan was furious, but his parents did not give in.

Evan gradually improved. A few months later, he seemed back to normal. Evan and his family were grateful for the counselor's help.

Feeling angry from time to time is normal. Feeling angry all the time is not normal. If a person feels like a walking time bomb, his or her anger may need professional attention.

Out-of-Control Anger

Evan's anger was out of control. This kind of anger differs from normal anger. Out-of-control anger occurs more frequently, is felt more deeply, and lasts longer than normal anger.

Out-of-control anger is destructive. Some people with out-of-control anger turn their anger inward. They become withdrawn, hopeless, and despairing. Other people with out-of-control anger turn their anger outward. They are likely to destroy property or threaten others.

Causes of Out-of-Control Anger

Many things can cause out-of-control anger. A combination of causes may be responsible.

Physical and Emotional Abuse

People who have been physically or sexually abused may develop out-of-control anger. Repeated frustration, rejection, or other emotional abuse also can lead to excessive anger. For example, anger can build up in teens who are ridiculed or treated as outsiders.

Anger Management

"I get so angry I feel like I'm going to explode on whoever is near me. I feel myself tensing up. I actually see stars."
—Dennis, age 16

Environmental Stress

People living in noisy or crowded neighborhoods may develop out-of-control anger. Environmental stress may include living in a family in which a family member may be unemployed or have an addiction. Children and teens who grow up in violent, unpredictable families may act rageful. They see family members explode in anger. They wrongly believe that explosive anger is the way to communicate feelings.

JEN, AGE 13

Jen's dad gets furious at the drop of a hat. His anger is especially bad when he has been drinking. Jen has learned to stay clear of her dad when he is angry. She tiptoes around the house so she won't disturb him. Living this way is hard on Jen. She feels a lot of anger. Fortunately, she's getting help through Al-Anon. This organization helps families in which one or more members are addicted to alcohol.

Traumatic Experience

A traumatic experience or event may cause extreme anger. Children and teens may become angry over the divorce of their parents or the death of a family member. The traumatic experience may be a natural disaster such as a fire or flood. Losing a home and possessions can fill a person with grief and anxiety.

Chronic Illness

Anger may accompany chronic physical illnesses such as arthritis or diabetes. People with a chronic illness may feel anger at the constant pressure to control their disease.

Experts say that 2 to 4 percent of teens belong to the out-of-control anger category.

Mental Disorder

Deep anger is sometimes a symptom of a mental disorder. Anger also may be a sign of depression or an eating disorder. In rare cases, rageful behavior may result from a brain injury.

Signs of Out-of-Control Anger

Warning signs of out-of-control anger may be hard to spot in teens. A teen's anger may be part of normal development. However, here are some important patterns and changes in behavior:

- Increased nervousness and anxiety

- Withdrawal from activities that were previously enjoyed

- Difficulty eating and sleeping

- Drop in school performance

- Increased acting out and reckless behavior, such as fighting, skipping school, shoplifting, or using drugs

Getting Help

Teens with out-of-control anger need the help of anger therapists. These mental health professionals provide intense, ongoing therapy.

A teen may attend individual or group therapy sessions one or more times a week. The sessions can continue for several weeks or months.

Anger Management

Counseling usually can help a highly angry person move to a middle range of anger in about 8 to 10 weeks.

During therapy sessions, the therapist may try to find out why a teen is angry. The therapist will train the teen in anger-management techniques such as those in this book. Sometimes a doctor can prescribe medicine to help control anger.

The teen also may participate in an anger support group. Teens share their experiences with anger and talk about how they cope. A support group lets teens know that others have the same problem they have.

You or someone you know may need help managing anger. If so, talk with your parents, school counselor, or doctor. Ask them to help you find a counselor trained in anger management. You can check the list of Useful Addresses and Internet Sites at the end of this book as well. You also can find professional help in the phone book. You may find an expert who specifically helps teens in the sections for *Mental Health Services* or *Psychologists*.

Points to Consider

How would you convince someone with out-of-control anger to get professional help?

What stresses might cause a teen to become rageful?

What can schools do to help teens manage their anger?

Are there students in your school who you think are extremely angry? What might you do about this?

Chapter Overview

Responding to the anger of others is another aspect of anger management.

Certain ground rules should be in place before responding to an angry person. These include no violence, no mood-altering substances, and no attacks with words.

Remaining calm is one of the best ways to respond to an angry person. Active listening and paraphrasing also are important.

It is best not to fight back against, or even respond to, angry strangers.

Chapter **8**

When Others Are Angry

Managing your own anger is a continual process. Also, you will need to respond to the anger of others at times. You can use many of the same anger-management techniques in both situations.

Ground Rules

There are ground rules for responding to the anger of others. These rules are needed for good communication. They also help protect you. The chart on the next page describes some situations, along with your best response.

Public anger is a growing concern in the United States. Consider these facts:

More employers are sending their employees to anger-management classes.

More hospitals and community education centers are offering anger-management classes to the public.

More and more judges are giving some offenders a choice. Minor offenders can choose to go to jail or to anger-management classes. Programs allowing this kind of choice have tripled in the United States since 1990.

The Situation:	Your Best Response:
An angry person threatens to hit or harm you.	Say nothing. Get away. If someone strikes you, report it and get help. Physical abuse is not legal.
An angry person is clearly drunk or drugged.	Say: "We will talk when you are sober." Then leave. People under the influence of mood-altering substances cannot think clearly. They may grow more angry.
An angry person attacks you with words or puts you down.	Say: "I am willing to listen, but only if I am not being attacked." Attacks on your self-esteem can make you angry and defensive. If the attacks continue, walk away or ask the person to leave.

Anger breeds anger. One angry person can make everyone around him or her angry.

Communicating With an Angry Person

Sometimes a family member, a friend, or even a stranger may be angry with you. A family member or friend may be angry with someone else and want you to listen. In either case, your goal should be to solve the problem. Try not to let the other person's anger make you angry.

Calm the Other Person

You can calm the other person by staying calm yourself. It is hard to remain angry with someone who does not respond with anger. Try to get the other person to copy your mood. Take slow, deep breaths. Speak softly. Tell the person you understand that he or she is angry.

Sally works as a waitress in a family-style restaurant. Most of

SALLY, AGE 17

her customers are pleasant. However, last night she waited on a difficult man. Nothing Sally did pleased him. The man said she got his order wrong. Then he said she was so slow that his food was cold.

Sally felt a spurt of anger. She forced herself to be pleasant. She kept calm by repeating to herself, "The customer is always right." Finally the man calmed down. He ate his dinner, and Sally found a $5 tip when she cleared his dishes.

What can you do about school bullies?
Experts recommend the following:

Avoid them if possible. Walk away from those who bother you.

Use humor. Cracking a joke will throw them off stride.

Make friends. Loners may appear to be easy targets.

Do not attack with words or weapons. Attacking will only make things worse.

Watch Your Body Language

Don't use body language that might seem aggressive. For example, do not lean forward. Step back to give the angry person plenty of room. Sit or stand still, with your hands at your sides.

Use Active Listening

Ask the other person to explain calmly why he or she is mad. Then listen without interrupting. Show that you are listening by nodding and maintaining eye contact. When the person is done speaking, paraphrase his or her message. Repeat in your own words what you heard the person say to you.

Solve the Problem

Once you know the problem, you can seek a solution. An apology may be all that is needed. By now, the other person may be ready to listen to your side of the story. When you are both calm and thinking clearly, come up with as many solutions as you can. Decide on the best one and try it. If that solution does not work, try another.

Remember, some problems do not have solutions. If this is the case, accept it and move on. Think about what you learned.

Tran and Lee were watching a movie at a theater. A telephone rang. They realized that the woman behind them had a cell phone. Tran and Lee asked her to take her call in the lobby. The woman replied angrily that she would not. The boys decided to move to different seats.

TRAN AND LEE, AGE 14

Stranger Anger

The best way to respond to an angry person you do not know is to keep cool and walk away. Take some deep breaths. You might even be extra polite to the next stranger you meet. Maybe your good manners will rub off on others.

Points to Consider

Do you think people show more anger in public now than in the past? Why or why not?

How would you respond to a child who is having a temper tantrum?

Describe a time when someone was angry with you. How did you handle the situation? What was the outcome?

Glossary

adrenaline (uh-DREN-uh-lin)—a chemical released from the adrenal glands when a person is angry

affirmation (af-ur-MAY-shuhn)—approval; a positive statement about oneself.

aggressive (uh-GRESS-iv)—behavior that is fierce or threatening; people with aggressive anger act out their feelings, often in an explosive manner.

assertive (uh-SUR-tiv)—able to stick up for oneself; people with assertive anger express their feelings in a calm, reasonable way.

chronic (KRON-ik)—lasting a long time

disability (diss-uh-BIL-i-tee)—something that makes a person lack the power to do something in the usual way

empathy (EM-puh-thee)—ability to understand the experiences and feelings of others

frustration (fruhss-TRAY-shuhn)—the feeling of discouragement when something prevents a person from doing something he or she tries

hormone (HOR-mohn)—a chemical produced by a gland; hormones control body functions and how a person grows or feels.

irrational (i-RASH-uh-nuhl)—unreasonable; not logical.

mediator (MEE-dee-ay-tuhr)—a person who helps two opposing sides settle a dispute

paraphrase (PA-ruh-fraze)—to restate something in your own words

passive (PASS-iv)—not fighting back or resisting; people with passive anger keep their feelings hidden.

sarcastic (sar-KASS-tik)—bitter or mocking; a sarcastic person means to hurt or make fun of someone or something.

therapy (THER-uh-pee)—treatment for an illness or a problem

For More Information

Cullen, Murray, and Joan Wright. *Cage Your Rage for Teens.* Lanham, MD: American Correctional Association, 1996.

Dentemaro, Christine, and Rachel Kranz. *Straight Talk About Anger.* New York: Facts on File, 1995.

Gregson, Susan R. *Stress Management.* Mankato, MN: Capstone Press, 2000.

Rawls, Bea O'Donnell. *Drugs and Anger.* Center City, MN: Hazelden, 1997.

Wilde, Jerry. *Hot Stuff to Help Kids Chill Out: The Anger Management Book.* Richmond, IN: LGR Publishing, 1997.

Useful Addresses and Internet Sites

Al-Anon Family Group Headquarters, Inc.
World Service Office
1600 Corporate Landing Parkway
Virginia Beach, VA 23454
1-800-356-9996
www.Al-Anon-Alateen.org

American Psychological Association
750 1st Street Northeast
Washington, DC 20002-4242
1-800-658-8994
www.apa.org/pubinfo/anger.html

National Mental Health Association
1021 Prince Street
Alexandria, VA 22314
1-800-969-6642
www.nmha.org/infoctr/factsheets/44.cfm

The Self-Help Resource Centre of Greater
Toronto
40 Orchard View Boulevard, Suite 219
Toronto, ON M4R 1B9
CANADA

The Christophers
www.christophers.org/angernn.html
News Note #408 provides teens with advice
on "getting a grip" when angry

Covenant House Nineline
1-800-999-9999 (24 hours)
Provides counseling for teens and parents

National Mental Health Net
www.mentalhelp.net
Type the word *anger* in the search line for
extensive links to Internet information on this
topic

Talk, Trust and Feel Therapeutics
www.members.aol.com/AngriesOut
Helps children, teens, and adults learn in an
upbeat, positive way how to deal with anger
and express it in a safe, constructive manner

Index